SIMPLE Peace
—— *in Philippians*

— STEVE YOUNG —

Copyright © 2014 by Steven M. Young
All rights reserved under International and Pan-American Copyright Conventions. This book or any portion thereof may not be reproduced or used in any manner whatsoever without the express written permission of the publisher except for the use of brief quotations in a book review.

First Printing, 2014

ISBN-13: 978-1502404718
ISBN-10: 1502404710

Published by: YesBear Publishing
3260 E. Lake Drive
Nashville TN 37214

Cover design: Mark Parq (www.markparq.com)

www.facebook.com/SIMPLEPeaceinPhilippians

Author available for speaking and coaching

CONTACT INFO:
Steve Young with *Good Tree Life Tools*
steve@GoodTreeLifeTools.com

Contents

Who Will Benefit From This Book?	4
Why Study Philippians…For Four Weeks?	5
Instructions for Your Experience	6
How to Use the SIMPLE Journal	7
The Book of Philippians (Daily Divisions)	11
Week One: The Stress of Life	13
Week Two: The Example to Follow	29
Week Three: The Motive to Continue	45
Week Four: The Peace of God	61
Group Study Guide	77
What? Memorize Scripture?	83
In Conclusion	87

Who Will Benefit From This Book?

Those who want to investigate Christianity on their own.

You're not sure what you believe about Christianity. You want a chance to read the Bible with an unbiased eye; to learn straight from the book and not from a person.

Those who feel the Bible is too difficult to understand.

You've been led to believe only the "professionals" can understand what the Bible means. You want to take the intimidation and confusion out of reading it.

Those who have lost the "umph" to their Christian life.

Your spiritual life isn't what it was in days past. You want a guide to help you re-establish your zeal for the simple truths in the Bible.

Those who want to immerse themselves deeply in the Bible one book at a time.

You've read other devotional books before which have helped you grow spiritually. Now, you want to dig deeper into the scriptures to see what you can learn yourself.

Why Study Philippians...For Four Weeks?

Paul originally wrote Philippians from prison to encourage his friends and fellow believers in Philippi. He wanted to show them the joy he had found which superseded all his terrible circumstances. His focus was on Christ alone and since that relationship could not be taken from him, all was well with the world! His message to his Philippian friends is applicable to us today. You will learn some amazing truths by looking over Paul's shoulder as he writes.

If you haven't read the Bible much before, the process set down in this book will help you experience something great. It will remove the intimidation you feel about reading the Bible on your own. You can choose one of three levels of intensity, *a la* KFC— *Regular*, *Crispy*, or *Extra-Crispy*!

Regular – Reading Only. Read all the Bible passages indicated each day and then the written commentary. Speak to God before and after for Him to show you things about your own life.

Crispy – Reading Plus Writing. Read all the indicated passages and commentary, and then interact with the verses by completing the SIMPLE Journaling technique. Pray before and after as well.

Extra-Crispy – Reading, Writing, & Memorizing – Read the passages and commentary, complete the SIMPLE Journal section, and memorize the selected verses from each chapter—two each week. See the article *What? Memorize Scripture?* (p. 83) for a helpful system. Incorporate prayer in and throughout everything.

After following this guide for four weeks, you will have mastered a process you can use for any book of the Bible. I encourage you to choose another book of the Bible next—perhaps Ephesians—and spend several weeks using this method for your study. I promise; it will change your life!

Steve Young
Nashville, Tennessee
October 2014

Instructions for Your Experience

Each week you will work your way through a chapter of Philippians; 4 weeks—4 chapters. Here are some suggestions to make your time alone with the Bible more meaningful and rich.

- ✟ The first Sunday you begin your study (and every Sunday thereafter), *read the entire book* of *Philippians through in a single sitting*. It will take you probably 15-20 minutes. Don't rush; enjoy the reading. Refer to the outline on page 11 as you read the first time. Remember that Philippians was originally a personal letter from a friend to his friends, and did not have chapter divisions and verses until later. This first step will be invaluable for you to understand the complete flow of the book.

- ✟ *Pray to God first each day asking for instruction and for your eyes to be open.* You may pray something like this:
  "God, as I read today, show me how to live my life better. Open my eyes to see and believe the truth."

- ✟ *Read the chapter of the week each day* (except Sunday because you will have just read the entire book!). During week one, you'll read chapter one each day. During week two, chapter two, and so forth. You will see the focal verses of the day's study in the broader context of the whole chapter. After four weeks, you will have read the entire book over 10 times!

- ✟ *Read again the focal verses for the day* while noting the main idea Paul presents. Don't run too quickly to the commentary. Decide on a main theme yourself and pick up any personal lessons you can. You may jot an idea in the ***P****hrase* section of the SIMPLE journal page for the day.

- ✟ *Read the commentary.* Consider it one person's ideas designed to give your own thought process a jump start! As you read, pay attention to what God is showing you.

- ✟ *Use the SIMPLE journaling method to interact with the passage.* Follow all six steps. Don't be afraid of the ***M****editation* portion; it could be the most profound of all!

- ✟ *End your time in prayer committing to God that you will follow His guidance today.* Find at least one very specific and tangible way you can *act* on what you've learned today.

How to Use the SIMPLE Journal

"I can't understand the Bible! It's too complicated!" Either you've heard someone say this, or you were the person saying it! The Bible is a love letter written by a Father to His children. The Father doesn't write to confuse His children but rather to instruct them in the best way of life. But for those who have not read the Bible on their own, it can certainly be intimidating. I guarantee this SIMPLE method will "de-intimidate" you!

When I read the Bible for myself, I believe God is even in control of what I chose to read in His word that day. I ask myself, "Why did God have me read this today? At this point in my life, what do I need to learn from Him?" He wants you to understand what you're reading more than you do! Listen to Him.

As you begin this 4-week journey through the book of Philippians, you'll interact profoundly with each section of the book you read. The SIMPLE steps will help in that interaction. We'll use the word "simple" as a guide for the six-step process:

> **S**elect
> **I**nvestigate
> **M**editate
> **P**hrase
> **L**ist
> **E**xpress

*S*elect

Select and write out the verse or parts of a verse that "wow-ed" you! Don't skip this part, and don't just write the reference! Writing out each word will cement God's idea to your mind. And while you are writing, He can give you more insight. Slow down. Write out the Scripture.

*I*nvestigate

What is going on in this text? What does the writer want the original readers to know? Then ask yourself, what is God is saying to you in this Scripture? Write it down in your own words. Ask the Holy Spirit to teach you the truth of His Word.

*M*editate

Next, put your pen down for a moment and visualize this truth in your mind. Determine what kind of images will drive home this principle. Draw what is in your mind. You don't have to be an artist; this is only for you!

*P*hrase

What is the main theme you are understanding today? Write out a phrase or statement which expresses this theme. (Think of a sound bite, or a Facebook quote). This phrase could serve as a caption to the meditation drawing you just completed.

*L*ist

List up to three ways to apply the idea to your own life. Personalize what you have read by asking yourself how it applies to your life right now. It may be instruction, encouragement, or a needed correction for you personally.

*E*xpress

This step is the most powerful part of the process. Express a written prayer. Share your heart with God. It can be as simple as asking Him to help you live out this Scripture. It might be praising Him for the truth you've learned. It might be a cry for help! Whatever your prayer is this day, write it out.

A SIMPLE Journal page for your use accompanies each day's reading. You'll find an example on the next page. If you see this page doesn't afford you enough room to write what you'd like, you have several options. You may want to buy a small notebook to use or purchase *My SIMPLE Journal* which I've designed for just this purpose.

Select – *Write out the verse (or part of a verse) you selected.*
Always offering prayer with joy in my every prayer for you all. —v. 4

Investigate – *What do you find in this verse?*
Paul prays frequently for the Philippians using words like "always", "every", and "you all." It's not a once in a while prayer.

Meditate – *What image comes to mind from the passage?*

Phrase – *What is the main theme or statement?*
Paul prays much and often for the Philippians.

List – *Actions you can take because of what you read*
I want to pray every day (and all through the day) for my wife, son, and daughter's.

Express – *Write out your prayer to God.*
Lord, thank you that you are so near and always accessible in prayer. Help me to pray each day this week for my family.

The Book of Philippians
(Daily Divisions)

Chapter 1:
The Stress of Life

Peace with God (1-2)
God's Reputation (3-5)
Confidence (6)
Prayer Life (7-11)
Difficult Rejoicing (12-20)
Priorities (21-26)
Choose Your Battles (27-2:2)

Chapter 2:
The Example to Follow

True Humility (3-4)
Christlike Attitudes (5)
Obedience (6-8)
He Knows Me! (9-11)
Changing Me (12-13)
Blamelessness (14-18)
Servanthood (19-30)

Chapter 3:
The Motive to Continue

Repetition (1)
False Confidence (2-6)
Christ Over All Else (7-8)
True Righteousness (9-11)
Don't Look Back (12-14)
Follow In Line (15-17)
Transformation (18-21)

Chapter 4:
The Peace of God

Harmony with Others (1-3)
A Gentle Spirit (4-5)
Peace of Mind (6-7)
Thoughts & Actions (8-9)
Contentment (10-14)
Giving & Givers (15-19)
Glory & Grace (20-23)

Week One

Philippians

Chapter 1
The Stress of Life

For it has been granted to you
on behalf of Christ
not only to believe in him,
but also to suffer for him,
since you are going through
the same struggle you saw I had,
and now hear that I still have.
(1:29-30)

Peace with God ____/____/____ **Sunday**

Read the entire book of Philippians
Read Focal Passage: Philippians 1:1-2
*Begin memorizing Phil. 1:6 and 1:21**

Write Philippians 1:6 out in full below.

_____

_____

_____

_____

    Paul's greeting is a common one in Christian writings, "Grace to you and peace from God." The irony comes when we realize the author writes this letter about joy and peace from a prison cell where most would not experience much peace. Even from his depressing situation, Paul wishes peace for his readers. Later in the letter, he explains this peace is unintelligible by most because it is not a feeling drummed up from within, but rather a deep trust in the character and might of his God.

    Are you feeling restless and uneasy, unsure about the future or in the middle of a crisis? This peace from God can transform your depression to exhilaration, your uncertainty to confidence, your fear for yourself to love for those around you. Peace comes when we know God more and believe His promise *never to leave or forsake us* (Deut. 31:6). The way to know God more is to read and chew on (meditate on) His love letter to His children, the Bible. May this four-week devotional through every verse of Philippians help you begin or continue that journey.

"God cannot give us a happiness and peace apart from Himself, because it is not there. There is no such thing." –C.S. Lewis

---

* See *What? Memorize Scripture?* on page 83 for helpful suggestions.

Select – *Write out the verse (or part of a verse) you selected.*

_____
_____
_____

Investigate – *What do you find in this verse?*

_____
_____
_____

Meditate – *What image comes to mind from the passage?*

Phrase – *What is the main theme or statement?*

_____
_____

List – *Actions you can take because of what you read*

_____
_____

Express – *Write out your prayer to God.*

_____
_____
_____

God's Reputation   ____/____/____ **Monday**

Read Philippians 1
Read Focal Passage: Philippians 1:3-5
Memorize Phil. 1:6 and 1:21

Write as much as you can of Philippians 1:6 looking at your Bible as little as possible.

_____

_____

_____

    I have a small business which provides a service to its customers. One of the main reasons it's doing well is because we have great reviews on several websites. Our reputation is one of consistent quality and honest service. Our past performance drives our future clients' confidence in us.

    In these verses, Paul remembers with the Philippians their partnership with him back when he was in their city. He indicates that now, when he speaks with God about them, his heart lifts because of these memories. He knows God did some great things in their lives during that time, and he's confident God will continue to work in and through them in the future.

    I encourage you to think through your past memories. Focus especially on those times God was very real to you; perhaps He helped you through a very difficult time. He was faithful then, and since God never changes, you can be confident He'll be faithful in the future. You can eagerly anticipate what He's going to teach you tomorrow.

"With true gratitude there is such a delight in the worth of God's past grace, that we are driven on to experience more and more of it in the future." – John Piper, Future Grace

Select – *Write out the verse (or part of a verse) you selected.*

_____
_____
_____

Investigate – *What do you find in this verse?*

_____
_____
_____

Meditate – *What image comes to mind from the passage?*

Phrase – *What is the main theme or statement?*

_____
_____

List – *Actions you can take because of what you read*

_____
_____

Express – *Write out your prayer to God.*

_____
_____
_____

Confidence   ___/___/___ ***Tuesday***

Read Philippians 1
Read Focal Passage: Philippians 1:6
Memorize Phil. 1:6 and 1:21

Write out Philippians 1:6 from memory.

_____
_____
_____
_____

For I am confident of this very thing, that He who began a good work in you will perfect it until the day of Christ Jesus. – New American Standard Version

Try this: say that verse out loud very slowly, listening to each and every word. Did you do it? Good! Now think about these questions: In whom is Paul confident? What is the "good work"? What is "the day of Christ Jesus"? Who began the work? Who will finish it?

Paul has a bold confidence in his praying. His confidence isn't based on the behavior of the Philippians, but rather on God's faithfulness. Paul has seen God do incredible things in Philippi (see Acts 16). He knows God never has a wasted action, so God will complete every project He begins. And God's projects will only be complete according to His own timetable.

If God has begun to work in your life, He will continue it until the end. His desire is to transform you more and more each day into the image of His Son, Jesus, but it takes a while. Be patient with yourself; be patient with those for whom you are praying. God is at work, but His time table may differ from yours.

He's still working on me to make me what I ought to be.
It took Him just a week to make the moon and stars,
The sun and the moon and Jupiter and Mars.
How loving and patient He must be, He's still working on me.
— *Joel Hemphill,* He's Still Working On Me *(children's song)*

S elect – *Write out the verse (or part of a verse) you selected.*

_____
_____
_____

I nvestigate – *What do you find in this verse?*

_____
_____
_____

M editate – *What image comes to mind from the passage?*

P hrase – *What is the main theme or statement?*

_____
_____

L ist – *Actions you can take because of what you read*

_____
_____

E xpress – *Write out your prayer to God.*

_____
_____
_____

Prayer Life

_____/_____/_____ **Wednesday**

Read Philippians 1
Read Focal Passage: Philippians 1:7-11
Memorize Phil. 1:6 and 1:21

Write Philippians 1:21 out in full below.

_____
_____
_____
_____

"Now I lay me down to sleep…" "Bless Mommy, and Daddy…"

Perhaps you've grown past these types of prayers, but how do you pray for others? Do you just ask God to "bless" them, keep them safe, and make them prosperous?

Because of his deep love for the Philippians (v. 7-8), Paul prayed specifically for them to grow in love (v. 9a), in wisdom (v. 9b-10a), and in obedience (v. 10b). He knew the only way this could happen was if they were first filled with Christ's righteousness (v.11a). He also knew this would result in God's own glory and praise (v.11b).

So what about us? How should we pray for others? To begin with, perhaps you can adopt Paul's outline here for your own prayers. When you pray for someone, try asking God to help them grow in love, wisdom and obedience, so that their lives glorify Him. Why would God not answer this prayer? Next, look for other qualities in their lives which, if developed, could result in God's glory; add them to your prayer list.

1 John 5:14-15 says "…if we ask anything according to His will, He hears us … [and] we know that we have the requests which we have asked from Him." What better confidence could we have? We can know without a doubt our prayers will be answered because we are asking for what God already wants to happen.

"Prayer is not overcoming God's reluctance, but laying hold of his willingness." – Martin Luther

Select – *Write out the verse (or part of a verse) you selected.*

_____
_____
_____

Investigate – *What do you find in this verse?*

_____
_____
_____

Meditate – *What image comes to mind from the passage?*

Phrase – *What is the main theme or statement?*

_____
_____

List – *Actions you can take because of what you read*

_____
_____

Express – *Write out your prayer to God.*

_____
_____
_____

Difficult Rejoicing ____/____/____ *Thursday*

Read Philippians 1
Read Focal Passage: Philippians 1:12-20
Memorize Phil. 1:6 and 1:21

Write as much as you can of Philippians 1:21 looking at your Bible as little as possible.

_____

_____

_____

_____

When my daughter was young, she stated quite sincerely, "Daddy, I really never have understood eternity." How would you have answered this question for an eight-year-old?

Paul has just told the Philippians about some distressing circumstances. How can he say, "I rejoice?" He can rejoice because he has an eternal perspective. It allows him to see his personal circumstances (v. 12-14), the work of other Christians (v. 15-18), and his own life or death (v. 19-20) in light of eternity.

Part of my answer to Audrey was this question, "In 50 years, what will it matter if you've lost your quarter?" What are your constant worries? Bills? Work projects? Upcoming events? What will they matter in 50 years? What will they matter in eternity? No one ever said on their deathbed, "I wish I'd spent more time at the office, instead of with my family!"

Someone once said, "If you're worrying about it, why pray? If you're praying about it, why worry?" Decide today: replace easy worrying with difficult rejoicing.

Worrying never robs tomorrow of its sorrow, it only saps today of its joy. – Leo Buscaglia

Select – *Write out the verse (or part of a verse) you selected.*

_____
_____
_____

Investigate – *What do you find in this verse?*

_____
_____
_____

Meditate – *What image comes to mind from the passage?*

Phrase – *What is the main theme or statement?*

_____
_____

List – *Actions you can take because of what you read*

_____
_____

Express – *Write out your prayer to God.*

_____
_____
_____

Priorities

____/____/____ **Friday**

Read Philippians 1
Read Focal Passage: Philippians 1:21-26
Memorize Phil. 1:6 and 1:21

Write out Philippians 1:21 from memory.

_____
_____
_____
_____

Seen the old comedy routine of Abbott & Costello, "Who's on First?" If you haven't, you owe it to yourself to find it on YouTube. Get ready for a belly laugh! Let me take a different twist here by asking, "Who *is* first?"

Paul has weighed this question carefully, and determined to place his own desires last. The bent of his life is to always glorify Christ—"to live is Christ"—so he decides to focus not on what is best for himself but what is best for the Philippians. He puts his own desires in the backseat.

I ask you, for whom are you living? What factors go into your decision-making? First, ask yourself if glorifying Jesus is your highest priority? Secondly, are you thinking about how you can glorify Him by helping others around you?

A Sunday school acronym has helped me with this: J-O-Y, which stands for **J**esus, **O**thers, and **Y**ou. It's a schematic for priorities in prayer and life focus. Is your life congruent with the JOY priorities?

"The momentary appeal of [selfish] tasks seems irresistible and they devour our energy. But in the light of time's perspective their deceptive prominence fades. With a sense of loss we recall the [others-focused] task we pushed aside. We realize we've become slaves to the tyranny of the urgent." --Charles E. Hummel

Philippians 1

Select – *Write out the verse (or part of a verse) you selected.*

_____
_____
_____

Investigate – *What do you find in this verse?*

_____
_____
_____

Meditate – *What image comes to mind from the passage?*

Phrase – *What is the main theme or statement?*

_____
_____

List – *Actions you can take because of what you read*

_____
_____

Express – *Write out your prayer to God.*

_____
_____
_____

Choose Your Battles ____/____/____ *Saturday*

Read Philippians 1
Read Focal Passage: Philippians 1:27-2:2
Memorize Phil. 1:6 and 1:21

Write out both Philippians 1:6 & 1:21 from memory.

I speak to parents often about how they raise their children. Most parents want their children to do and be good. As a result, it's difficult for them to refrain from pointing out every little thing the child does wrong. As a result, the child gets overwhelmed and defensive, then stops responding to any of their instructions.

I encourage parents with today's principle: Choose Your Battles. If they are battling against messy rooms and taking drugs with the same veracity, something is wrong!

Paul encourages the Philippians to be unified by "standing firm in one spirit, with one mind striving together for the faith of the gospel." The church should be more concerned with the larger issues instead of squabbling about trivial matters.

What was your last argument about? Don't let something that doesn't matter cause you to lose something that does.

In necessary things, unity; in doubtful things, liberty; in all things, charity. –Richard Baxter

Select – *Write out the verse (or part of a verse) you selected.*

_____

_____

_____

Investigate – *What do you find in this verse?*

_____

_____

_____

Meditate – *What image comes to mind from the passage?*

Phrase – *What is the main theme or statement?*

_____

_____

List – *Actions you can take because of what you read*

_____

_____

Express – *Write out your prayer to God.*

_____

_____

_____

Week Two

Philippians

Chapter 2
The Example to Follow

In your relationships with one another,
have the same mindset
as Christ Jesus.
(2:5)

True Humility   ____/____/____ **Sunday**

Read the entire book of Philippians
Read Focal Passage: Philippians 2:3-4
Begin memorizing Phil. 2:3 and 2:13

Write out Philippians 2:3 below.

_____

_____

_____

_____

Our family enjoys movies. In fact, part of our family culture is using our favorite movie quotes in everyday conversation. One much-used quote is from the movie *Finding Nemo*, where birds are the mindless enemies of the fish world. Seagulls are only heard to say one thing, "Mine-mine-mine-mine!"

Not surprisingly, this word was the first word for many of us! "Mine!" The same concept shows up in witticisms of the day. "Look out for number one!" "Get what you can, can all you get, and sit on the can!"

Humility is not a naturally occurring attitude; it must be developed. Being humble goes against every force in our nature. Personal survival is primary. The character quality for which we must strive is "others-centeredness." Even when we try to be humble, we are focused on ourselves. Richard Whately said, "A man is called selfish not for pursuing his own good, but for neglecting his neighbor's."

John Bunyan said, "You have not lived until you have done something for someone who can never repay you."

"In reality, there is, perhaps, no one of our natural passions so hard to subdue as pride....For, even if I could conceive that I had completely overcome it, I should probably be proud of my humility."
– Benjamin Franklin

Select – *Write out the verse (or part of a verse) you selected.*

_____
_____
_____

Investigate – *What do you find in this verse?*

_____
_____
_____

Meditate – *What image comes to mind from the passage?*

Phrase – *What is the main theme or statement?*

_____
_____

List – *Actions you can take because of what you read*

_____
_____

Express – *Write out your prayer to God.*

_____
_____
_____

Christlike Attitudes ___/___/___ *Monday*

Read Philippians 2
Read Focal Passage: Philippians 2:5
Memorize Phil. 2:3 and 2:13

Write as much as you can of Philippians 2:3 looking at your Bible as little as possible.

_____

_____

_____

_____

WWJD bracelets were all the rage several years ago. Though the message was a bit overused, the process of measuring my decisions against those Jesus would make in my situation is a sound one. What would Jesus do if he were in my shoes?

Verse 5 speaks directly about this attitude of humility with Paul's injunction before and Christ's example following. Are there other attitudes we should adopt as well? Other verses in the Bible repeat the idea that Jesus' example is one to follow: "The one who says he abides in Him ought himself to walk in the same manner as He walked" (1 John 2:6).

I may agree Jesus' attitudes are ones to emulate, but how do I know what attitudes to target? How can I imitate anyone? I must first study the life of the one I'm following. I must put in the effort to read the stories, learn about His life, and allow the Holy Spirit to point out areas to correct in my own life. In this way, I will constantly be transformed into the image of my Big Brother, Jesus (Rom. 8:14-17).

"For you have been called for this purpose, since Christ also suffered for you, leaving you an example for you to follow in his steps." – 1 Peter 2:21

Select – *Write out the verse (or part of a verse) you selected.*

_____
_____
_____

Investigate – *What do you find in this verse?*

_____
_____
_____

Meditate – *What image comes to mind from the passage?*

Phrase – *What is the main theme or statement?*

_____
_____

List – *Actions you can take because of what you read*

_____
_____

Express – *Write out your prayer to God.*

_____
_____
_____

Obedience   ____/____/____ *Tuesday*

Read Philippians 2
Read Focal Passage: Philippians 2:6-8
Memorize Phil. 2:3 and 2:13

Write out Philippians 2:3 from memory.

_____

_____

_____

_____

Growing up, our family had two German shepherds named Mutt & Jeff. Though brothers, Jeff was obviously the more intelligent dog. My mother said, "Mutt is the only dog who ever failed obedience school!"

It is difficult for any of us to be obedient. We do not believe any authority could have our best interests at heart. We have never experienced a boss or governmental leader who consistently put the well-being of his employees or constituents first.

Jesus "*learned obedience* from the things which He suffered" (Heb. 5:8). Jesus suffered most during the crucifixion and before, in the Garden of Gethsemane. In these moments, Jesus knew his Father's will was primary, though different from His own (see Matt. 26:39). Jesus' desire was to escape the cross ("let this cup pass from Me"), but he submitted his own will to the will of his Father. Think about this: *Jesus obeyed his Father's will even though he had a different and opposing will.*

This tells me several things. Since Jesus never sinned, his desire to do something different than what the Father proposed was *not* a sin. The sin would have been to disobey the Father. But instead *Jesus made his own desires subservient to the Father's desires.* Jesus obeyed the Father even though he didn't agree with the plan! So, I must obey the Father's will even when I don't understand it or agree with it.

"*Behold, to obey is better than sacrifice.*" – 1 Samuel 15:22

Select – *Write out the verse (or part of a verse) you selected.*

_____
_____
_____

Investigate – *What do you find in this verse?*

_____
_____
_____

Meditate – *What image comes to mind from the passage?*

Phrase – *What is the main theme or statement?*

_____
_____

List – *Actions you can take because of what you read*

_____
_____

Express – *Write out your prayer to God.*

_____
_____
_____

He Knows Me! ____/____/____ **Wednesday**

Read Philippians 2
Read Focal Passage: Philippians 2:9-11
Memorize Phil. 2:3 and 2:13

Write out Philippians 2:13 below.

"Guess who I saw in the airport!" My wife, Laura, had just been on a trip where she had seen from a distance a top-level government figure. Having not been around "celebrities" much, this was a high point in our life, being so close to someone of such renown.

Today's scripture describes One of renown whom I can know intimately; but even more incredible—He knows me intimately! This God-man was exalted by his Father above all others, yet He calls me one of His own.

I picture one amazing day when all "in heaven and earth and under the earth" will bow in humble submission to the One who created them. I will be in the crowd that day and I will look past them all to see the familiar face of One who knows me. As He quietly receives the adulation of the multitude, I see Him looking over their heads until He catches my eye. He smiles, and…did He just do what I think He did? Yes, He winked at me!

If I could know a single ant, his family, his struggles, his very thoughts; it would not be any greater than Jesus' loving interest in me and my life. O, what a wonderful Savior I have!

Jesus knows me this I love.
No, I'll never understand.
How He could see the heart of me,
And want me just the way I am.
Jesus knows me this I love. —Morgan Easter

Select – *Write out the verse (or part of a verse) you selected.*

_____
_____
_____

Investigate – *What do you find in this verse?*

_____
_____
_____

Meditate – *What image comes to mind from the passage?*

Phrase – *What is the main theme or statement?*

_____
_____

List – *Actions you can take because of what you read*

_____
_____

Express – *Write out your prayer to God.*

_____
_____
_____

Changing Me   ____/____/____ *Thursday*

Read Philippians 2
Read Focal Passage: Philippians 2:12-13
Memorize Phil. 2:3 and 2:13

Write as much as you can of Philippians 2:13 looking at your Bible as little as possible.

_____

_____

_____

"But I don't wanna!" How many parents have heard this declaration from our children? How many of us remember saying this as a child? As I mature, I may not say it out loud anymore, but it's often still true in my heart; sadly, even regarding the direction I receive from God.

The truth is I will never *naturally* want to do what God wants me to do. To obey God is *super*-natural; my bent is to follow my own desires, not the desires of any other. I want…what I want…when I want it!

Today's passage says God is working in me to change my will—to change my "wannas"—so that I will *wanna* work for His good pleasure—not my own. God is changing me from the inside out to reshape my desires to match His own. He is helping me day by day to become more obedient.

The famous verse Psalm 37:4 says, "Delight yourself in the Lord and He will give you the desires of your heart." What if this verse means not that God will give me the objects of my desires, but that He will give me my actual desires? As I delight myself in the Lord, He will change my desires to be more in line with His own. More and more, I *want* to obey Him. I'll wanna do what He wants me to do! How about you?

"The way to conquer sin is not by working hard to change our deeds, but by trusting Jesus to change our desires. –David Platt

Philippians 2

Select – *Write out the verse (or part of a verse) you selected.*

_____
_____
_____

Investigate – *What do you find in this verse?*

_____
_____
_____

Meditate – *What image comes to mind from the passage?*

Phrase – *What is the main theme or statement?*

_____
_____

List – *Actions you can take because of what you read*

_____
_____

Express – *Write out your prayer to God.*

_____
_____
_____

Blamelessness   ____/____/____ *Friday*

Read Philippians 2
Read Focal Passage: Philippians 2:14-18
Memorize Phil. 2:3 and 2:13

Write out Philippians 2:13 from memory.

_____

_____

_____

_____

One of my daughters' favorite movies and book series is *The Princess Diaries*. It has a familiar theme: a young girl learns she is a royal heir, and she must learn to live in her new station and the culture of her grandmother. Hilarity ensues as their worlds collide.

When we become children of God (v. 15), we are not magically made holy like our Holy Father. We must learn how to live this new kingdom life as princes and princesses of the King of the universe.

These verses state we must forsake our old ways and be "blameless" and "innocent." Blameless means "free from or not deserving blame." It indicates we must be careful not to tarnish the reputation of our new Father and our new family. We must watch what we do and how we do it so no one has the chance to blame us for any wrong. Another way to say this is to be "above reproach."

One family motto we have is "Others may; I may not." I must choose to limit myself to those activities which are clearly upright and honest, with not even the slightest hint of evil regardless of what others around me may choose to do. My new Father deserves this from me. Consider your life today: What needs to change for you to be called blameless?

"Preach the gospel at all times, and when necessary, use words." -- *St. Francis of Assisi*

Philippians 2

Select – *Write out the verse (or part of a verse) you selected.*

_____
_____
_____

Investigate – *What do you find in this verse?*

_____
_____
_____

Meditate – *What image comes to mind from the passage?*

Phrase – *What is the main theme or statement?*

_____
_____

List – *Actions you can take because of what you read*

_____
_____

Express – *Write out your prayer to God.*

_____
_____
_____

Servanthood   ___/___/___   *Saturday*

Read Philippians 2
Read Focal Passage: Philippians 2:19-30
Memorize Phil. 2:3 and 2:13

Write out both Philippians 2:3 and 2:13 from memory.

How would you define the word "servanthood?" Paul writes that Timothy served him "like a child serving his father." What intimacy he conveys! A servant puts the needs of others before his own. Here we see the outgrowth of the true humility described earlier in verses 3 and 4. Servanthood is the demonstrated action of a humble person seeking the good of another.

It's easier to serve those we love; those who seem to deserve the service we offer. It's more difficult (seemingly impossible?) to serve those whom we deem undeserving. In these instances, we must look past the individual to the actual Receiver of our service: God Himself. We serve God through our service to others. How this looks in your life will be different from the way it looks in mine. Ask God to show you how and who to serve today.

The humble man looks upon every, the feeblest and unworthiest, child of God, and honors him and prefers him in honor as the son of a King. — Andrew Murray

S elect – *Write out the verse (or part of a verse) you selected.*

_____
_____
_____

I nvestigate – *What do you find in this verse?*

_____
_____
_____

M editate – *What image comes to mind from the passage?*

P hrase – *What is the main theme or statement?*

_____
_____

L ist – *Actions you can take because of what you read*

_____
_____

E xpress – *Write out your prayer to God.*

_____
_____
_____

Week Three

Philippians

Chapter 3
The Motive to Continue

Not that I have already obtained all this,
or have already arrived at my goal,
but I press on to take hold of
that for which Christ Jesus
took hold of me.
(3:12)

Repetition

_____/_____/_____ **Sunday**

Read the entire book of Philippians
Read Focal Passage: Philippians 3:1
Begin memorizing Phil. 3:7 and 3:14

Write out Philippians 3:7 below.

_____

_____

_____

_____

My wife loves Dollywood, an amusement park in the Smoky Mountains of Tennessee. I believe she would go there every weekend if it weren't four hours from our house. No matter how many times we repeat that trip, she loves it.

We only repeat things we view as valuable and important. In today's focal verse, Paul repeats some advice he's given the Philippians before: "Rejoice in the Lord." He's mentioned it earlier in this letter and will return to the same theme several more times before closing.

Why do those around us repeat advice they've given us before? Because they believe we don't yet understand its importance. Our lives are not producing the fruits that come from following their advice. They repeat themselves, at the risk of ridicule from us, because they feel the advice is a "safeguard" for us, just as Paul is doing here.

Do you wish they'd stop repeating? As soon as we consistently begin doing what they're advising, they will stop. When they feel they've gotten through to us and the information is our own, they will begin to trust we're on the right track.

What advice do you keep repeating? What advice do others continually give you? What needs to happen next?

"Repetition is the mother of learning."—Apache saying

Select – *Write out the verse (or part of a verse) you selected.*

_____
_____
_____

Investigate – *What do you find in this verse?*

_____
_____
_____

Meditate – *What image comes to mind from the passage?*

Phrase – *What is the main theme or statement?*

_____
_____

List – *Actions you can take because of what you read*

_____
_____

Express – *Write out your prayer to God.*

_____
_____
_____

False Confidence ____/____/____ **Monday**

Read Philippians 3
Read Focal Passage: Philippians 3:2-6
Memorize 3:7 and 3:14

Write as much as you can of Philippians 3:7 looking at your Bible as little as possible.

_____

_____

_____

_____

"I can do it myself!" The little boy attempts to reach up and put the empty glass on the countertop. His father reacts quickly and catches the glass just in time to catch it before it crashes to the floor.

We laugh at the immature confidence of small children; so confident they cannot fail that they are blind to the consequences only their parents can see. As adults, we attempt to increase our self-confidence with degrees, awards, and experience. Each item adds a building block to the edifice we build to ourselves. But Paul beat us all!

He has all the earthly qualifications one could want to bolster personal confidence. He describes it as "confidence in the flesh," his "former manner of life" (Eph. 4:22-24). Once he was "renewed in the spirit of [his] mind," he became dependent on God to give him confidence. As we see in verse 24, Paul's dependence resulted in his actions of "true righteousness and holiness."

Confidence is not wrong, but I must be sure my confidence is well-based. If I base it on myself and my experience alone, and I don't learn from others or God, I am doomed to a cyclical pattern of disappointment. But if my confidence comes from God (see Phil. 1:6 again), I'll experience amazing accomplishments as I walk through life.

"You never really learn much from hearing yourself speak." — George Clooney

Select – *Write out the verse (or part of a verse) you selected.*

_____
_____
_____

Investigate – *What do you find in this verse?*

_____
_____
_____

Meditate – *What image comes to mind from the passage?*

Phrase – *What is the main theme or statement?*

_____
_____

List – *Actions you can take because of what you read*

_____
_____

Express – *Write out your prayer to God.*

_____
_____
_____

SIMPLE Peace

Christ Over All Else ____/____/____ **Tuesday**

Read Philippians 3
Read Focal Passage: Philippians 3:7-8
Memorize 3:7 and 3:14

Write out Philippians 3:7 from memory.

_____

_____

_____

_____

As they grow older, many people begin to look carefully at the life they've lived and the choices they've made. Sadly, many reflect on their lives with regret. Several books and movies demonstrate a similar theme: Ebenezer Scrooge in *A Christmas Carol* and more recently Nicolas Cage's character in *Family Man*. When weighed on a true scale of worth, their frenzy of activity falls far short of the cost of what has been lost. The saying goes, "All my life, I've been climbing the ladder of success. Finally, when I reached the top, I looked around and realized the ladder was leaning against the wrong building!"

Paul had spent his life climbing the Jewish ladder of success. But now, in comparison to what he has found in Christ, he classifies his accomplishments as refuse (or garbage, dung, excrement, offscourings, dregs, what is thrown to dogs, worthless and detestable, filth). He says what he has found is of "surpassing value;" like the difference of choosing between a crayon, a stick of gum, or $100,000!

Ask yourself where you spend your time; the answer will tell you where your life's priorities lie. Then ask yourself, "What adjustments must I make?"

"Things which matter most must never be at the mercy of things which matter least." — Johann Wolfgang von Goethe

Philippians 3

Select – *Write out the verse (or part of a verse) you selected.*

_____
_____
_____

Investigate – *What do you find in this verse?*

_____
_____
_____

Meditate – *What image comes to mind from the passage?*

Phrase – *What is the main theme or statement?*

_____
_____

List – *Actions you can take because of what you read*

_____
_____

Express – *Write out your prayer to God.*

_____
_____
_____

True Righteousness ___/___/___ *Wednesday*

Read Philippians 3
Read Focal Passage: Philippians 3:9-11
Memorize 3:7 and 3:14

Write out Philippians 3:14 below.

_____

_____

_____

I remember being afraid when I read 1 Peter 1:16 in the old King James version of the Bible, where God says, "Be ye holy, for I am holy!" How could this be a fair command from God? How could God set up that standard of perfect righteousness for me to follow since He knows I'm not perfect like He is?

I remember later seeing with much relief today's passage, where in verse 9 we learn the way we are to acquire true righteousness. It says I come to God "not having a righteousness of my own" consequent to my following perfectly a set of rules, but this righteousness comes to me from God "on the basis of faith." What release! My faith, not my actions, is the determining factor (see also Eph. 2:8-9). I can come to God knowing that the perfect life Jesus lived on earth is credited to me, so my actions don't count against me in God's eyes.

Now, I am free to do good works and serve others out of gratitude to God for my salvation. What a difference than if I do good works motivated by the fear of what might happen if I don't! Jesus has traded his "robe of righteousness" (Isa. 61:10) for my "filthy rags" (Isa. 64:6)!

Perfect righteousness requires both perfect conduct and a perfect heart. But none of us rise to this standard. Our only hope is Christ. – Clyde Cranford, Because We Love Him *(p. 77)*

Select – *Write out the verse (or part of a verse) you selected.*

_____
_____
_____

Investigate – *What do you find in this verse?*

_____
_____
_____

Meditate – *What image comes to mind from the passage?*

Phrase – *What is the main theme or statement?*

_____
_____

List – *Actions you can take because of what you read*

_____
_____

Express – *Write out your prayer to God.*

_____
_____
_____

Don't Look Back

____/____/____ **Thursday**

Read Philippians 3
Read Focal Passage: Philippians 3:12-14
Memorize 3:7 and 3:14

Write as much as you can of Philippians 3:14 looking at your Bible as little as possible.

_____

_____

_____

_____

Curly: You know what the secret of life is?
Mitch: No, what?
Curly: This. [holds up one finger]
Mitch: Your finger?
Curly: One thing. Just one thing. You stick to that and everything else don't mean sh**.
Mitch: That's great, but what's the "one thing?"
Curly: That's what you've got to figure out. (*City Slickers* movie)

Most have not figured out what their "one thing" is, but Paul had; it was his prized relationship with Jesus. He said he "pressed on" toward the goal. How? By forgetting the past and moving toward the future. It's as if he says, "When I fail, I put it behind me, learn from it, and renew my efforts toward holiness!" In Luke 9:62 Jesus said, "No one, after putting his hand to the plow and looking back, is fit for the kingdom of God."

I do not spend a lot of energy replaying in my mind what I should have done. The past can be an anchor to future progress. Don't let it be! Determine the most important thing, and run toward it!

"Look back, learn much, and live well." – Steve Young

Select – *Write out the verse (or part of a verse) you selected.*

_____
_____
_____

Investigate – *What do you find in this verse?*

_____
_____
_____

Meditate – *What image comes to mind from the passage?*

Phrase – *What is the main theme or statement?*

_____
_____

List – *Actions you can take because of what you read*

_____
_____

Express – *Write out your prayer to God.*

_____
_____
_____

Follow in Line

_____/_____/_____ Friday

Read Philippians 3
Read Focal Passage: Philippians 3:15-17
Memorize 3:7 and 3:14

Write out Philippians 3:14 from memory.

_____

_____

_____

_____

"Line up, line up!" My elementary school teacher always made us form a single file line before we could go to lunch, recess, or anything else. I didn't like to line up; I wanted to run and play!

Paul uses a word in verse 16 which is translated "to live;"—"let us keep *living* by that same standard." It literally means "let us keep following in line." Paul wants the Philippians to follow his example and the example of those who "walk according to the pattern" he had established; those who had followed in line.

Each of us owes a debt of gratitude to those who have gone before us. I waste so many of my mistakes on things I could have learned from others. Am I so prideful to think I don't need input from other people?

Each of us needs a Paul (a mentor), a Barnabas (a friend), and a Timothy (one whom you can mentor). We are all in the line of faith. We need to follow the examples of others, provide an example for others to follow, and encourage others to do the same. Where are you in line, and who is with you? We all need each other.

"If I have seen further, it is by standing on the shoulders of giants." - *Sir Isaac Newton*

Select – *Write out the verse (or part of a verse) you selected.*

_____
_____
_____

Investigate – *What do you find in this verse?*

_____
_____
_____

Meditate – *What image comes to mind from the passage?*

Phrase – *What is the main theme or statement?*

_____
_____

List – *Actions you can take because of what you read*

_____
_____

Express – *Write out your prayer to God.*

_____
_____
_____

Transformation   ____/____/____ **Saturday**

Read Philippians 3
Read Focal Passage: Philippians 3:18-21
Memorize 3:7 and 3:14

Write out both Philippians 3:7 and 3:14 from memory.

_____

_____

_____

_____

_____

_____

_____

_____

     My wife and I coach people who want to learn to live healthier lives. We help them form a plan for eating and exercise so they move toward a healthy lifestyle. On their way, they lose weight and get more fit. We have learned that internal personal motivation is essential for the success of our program. No one can "want it" for someone else.

     Sadly, some churches attempt to change people by telling them what they can and cannot do. A list of rules is easier to teach and enforce than helping their members understand how to make godly choices. They are trying to make people conform to their rules from the outside in; but the Holy Spirit changes us from the inside out. Instead of promoting the rules, they should help their members follow the Spirit's guidance and He will lead them where they need to go. Like a caterpillar to a butterfly, He transforms us from within.

Gracefulness has been defined to be the outward expression of the inward harmony of the soul.—William Hazlitt

Select – *Write out the verse (or part of a verse) you selected.*

_____

_____

_____

Investigate – *What do you find in this verse?*

_____

_____

_____

Meditate – *What image comes to mind from the passage?*

Phrase – *What is the main theme or statement?*

_____

_____

List – *Actions you can take because of what you read*

_____

_____

Express – *Write out your prayer to God.*

_____

_____

_____

Week Four

Philippians

Chapter 4
The Peace of God

And the peace of God,
which transcends all understanding,
will guard your hearts
and your minds
in Christ Jesus.
(4:7)

Harmony with Others ____/____/____ *Sunday*

Read the entire book of Philippians
Read Focal Passage: Philippians 4:1-3
Begin memorizing Phil. 4:6 and 4:13

Write out Philippians 4:6 below.

_____

_____

_____

_____

A scene in the musical *The Music Man* depicts Professor Hill, the con artist, being accosted by four men from the school board. These men have "hated each other for 15 years!" and were always bickering with one other. Hill teaches them to sing, they become a barbershop quartet, and they never appear in the movie again except they are singing together.

As you have seen, one of Paul's favorite themes in this book is for the Philippians to "be of the same mind" (see 1:27; 2:2, 5). He knows the difficulties of living the Christian life and desires for them to help one another, and not waste their energies battling amongst themselves. He tells two women to "live in harmony" with one another.

To harmonize with one another means two people are singing, not the same notes, but rather that the notes are complimentary. They form a chord which is pleasant to the ear. Living in harmony doesn't mean being exactly alike, but being a help and not a hindrance to one another. Differences in personality and style make up the color and fragrance of a relationship, but only if each one appreciates the differences.

"Adversity draws men together and produces beauty and harmony in life's relationships, just as the cold of winter produces ice-flowers on the window-panes, which vanish with the warmth." — *Søren Kierkegaard*

Select – *Write out the verse (or part of a verse) you selected.*

_____
_____
_____

Investigate – *What do you find in this verse?*

_____
_____
_____

Meditate – *What image comes to mind from the passage?*

Phrase – *What is the main theme or statement?*

_____
_____

List – *Actions you can take because of what you read*

_____
_____

Express – *Write out your prayer to God.*

_____
_____
_____

SIMPLE Peace

A Gentle Spirit ____/____/____ **Monday**

Read Philippians 4
Read Focal Passage: Philippians 4:4-5
Memorize 4:6 and 4:13

Write as much as you can of Philippians 4:6 looking at your Bible as little as possible.

_____

_____

_____

_____

"Be a real man!" "Just man up!"—these familiar phrases are applied to men of today. Rarely do you see an injunction to acquire a "gentle spirit," or to have this be your reputation "known to all men."

A man (or woman) with a gentle spirit is confident because he doesn't have to prove himself to anyone; his self-identity is secure. He is approachable by all because he does not put on an arrogant air of superiority as a defense against hidden feelings of inadequacy or self-deceived competence.

When we first contemplated moving to Mexico as missionaries, I was very intimidated by the task. I did not feel adequate to do what God was asking us to do. Then He showed me this verse, "Not that we are adequate in ourselves to consider anything as coming from ourselves, but our adequacy is from God, who also made us adequate as servants…" (2 Cor. 3:5-6a). Resting in his power allows me to have a gentle spirit and serve others with confidence.

"The gentle overcomes the rigid. The slow overcomes the fast. The weak overcomes the strong… Everyone knows that the yielding overcomes the stiff, and the soft overcomes the hard. Yet no one applies this knowledge." — *Lao Tzu*

Select – *Write out the verse (or part of a verse) you selected.*

_____
_____
_____

Investigate – *What do you find in this verse?*

_____
_____
_____

Meditate – *What image comes to mind from the passage?*

Phrase – *What is the main theme or statement?*

_____
_____

List – *Actions you can take because of what you read*

_____
_____

Express – *Write out your prayer to God.*

_____
_____
_____

Peace of Mind   ____/____/____ **Tuesday**

Read Philippians 4
Read Focal Passage: Philippians 4:6-7
Memorize 4:6 and 4:13

Write out Philippians 4:6 from memory.

_____

_____

_____

_____

My mother-in-law has a running joke. She says, "You know how they say 90% of the things you worry about never happen? See, worrying works! Maybe if I hadn't worried, those things would have happened!"

Today's passage is the go-to verse for worrying. What are we anxious about? What do we worry about? Many worries have as their focus a situation or event in the future over which we have no control. It would seem that if we realized we had no control over it, we would let it go and just wait to see what happens. But we feel we must control our lives, so we worry.

Worry in the life of a Christian is an indication of a lack of trust. We don't trust that God is good or that God is all-powerful. If we believe these two facts, we wouldn't feel the need to worry.

Paul knows this and encourages the reader to "lay their burdens down." Entrust them to God and let him do what he does best—be in control.

Lay your burden down, lay your burden down.
Take your troubled soul, your tired mind and lay your burden down.
Lay your burden down, get your feet on solid ground.
Take your worries to the foot of the cross, and lay your burden down.
– Chuck Girard

Select – *Write out the verse (or part of a verse) you selected.*

_____
_____
_____

Investigate – *What do you find in this verse?*

_____
_____
_____

Meditate – *What image comes to mind from the passage?*

Phrase – *What is the main theme or statement?*

_____
_____

List – *Actions you can take because of what you read*

_____
_____

Express – *Write out your prayer to God.*

_____
_____
_____

Thoughts & Actions ___/___/___ *Wednesday*

Read Philippians 4
Read Focal Passage: Philippians 4:8-9
Memorize 4:6 and 4:13

Write out Philippians 4:13 below.

_____
_____
_____
_____

  Garbage in, garbage out (GIGO) is a term from the early dawn of computer technology. In short, it referred to the need to be careful in using programming languages, because any small error (garbage in) would result in some malfunction in the program (garbage out). This analogy works well with today's passage, too. It shows the link between thoughts and actions and feelings.

  We are bombarded with information from media, marketing, and advertising. Personal information overload is a very real problem. We must filter the information which enters our minds (input) because it will affect our actions (output). Verse 8 is a filter I use to monitor what goes into my mind. This filter helps my thoughts to be healthy. Then I attempt to "practice these things" (actions), with the result being a personal sense of peace from God (feelings).

  The gatekeeper of my life is my mind. Instead of GIGO, I want PIPO (purity in, purity out). What adjustments do you need to make for your input/output to be pure?

Your beliefs become your thoughts, your thoughts become your words, your words become your actions, your actions become your habits, your habits become your values, your values become your destiny. — *Mahatma Gandhi*

Philippians 4

Select – *Write out the verse (or part of a verse) you selected.*

_____
_____
_____

Investigate – *What do you find in this verse?*

_____
_____
_____

Meditate – *What image comes to mind from the passage?*

Phrase – *What is the main theme or statement?*

_____
_____

List – *Actions you can take because of what you read*

_____
_____

Express – *Write out your prayer to God.*

_____
_____
_____

Contentment   ____/____/____   **Thursday**

Read Philippians 4
Read Focal Passage: Philippians 4:10-14
Memorize 4:6 and 4:13

Write as much as you can of Philippians 4:13 looking at your Bible as little as possible.

_____

_____

_____

_____

"Just one more! Just one more!" Every parent has heard this phrase from their child. One more cookie, one more toy, one more turn on the merry-go-round and all will be well with the world. After the "one more" is given, the child begins a reprise of the "just one more" chorus! Just one more is never enough. We adults do the same thing: just one more sale, just one more car, just one more house. On and on it goes. When is "just one more" enough?

Paul has learned the secret to contentment. The secret is in Christ who strengthens him for all things. I must not concern myself with that which I cannot have at the moment, but rather enjoy that which I do have. I must also not fret about those things I cannot change; I must accept them and rest.

"He who is not contented with what he has, would not be contented with what he would like to have." — Socrates

"Be thankful for what you have; you'll end up having more. If you concentrate on what you don't have, you will never, ever have enough." — Oprah Winfrey

"For after all, the best thing one can do when it is raining is let it rain." — Henry Wadsworth Longfellow

Select – *Write out the verse (or part of a verse) you selected.*

_____
_____
_____

Investigate – *What do you find in this verse?*

_____
_____
_____

Meditate – *What image comes to mind from the passage?*

Phrase – *What is the main theme or statement?*

_____
_____

List – *Actions you can take because of what you read*

_____
_____

Express – *Write out your prayer to God.*

_____
_____
_____

Giving & Givers

_____/_____/_____ Friday

Read Philippians 4
Read Focal Passage: Philippians 4:15-19
Memorize 4:6 and 4:13

Write out Philippians 4:13 from memory.

_____

_____

_____

_____

The Philippians had proved their love for Paul by supporting his ministry financially time and time again. In Michael Card's song *Distressing Disguise*, he describes an amazing concept about giving and receiving. See if you can catch it.

> *Every time a faithful servant serves a brother that's in need, what happens at that moment is a miracle indeed. As they look to one another in an instant it is clear, Only Jesus is visible for they've both disappeared.*

> *He is in the hand that reaches out to give; He is in the touch that causes men to live. So speak with your life now as well as your tongue; shelter the homeless, take care of the young.*

> *In His distressing disguise He hopes that we'll realize that when we take care of the poorest of them, we've really done it to Him.*

When we give to others, they see the gift as coming to them from God himself. Jesus said, "To the extent that you did it to one of these brothers of Mine, even the least of them, you did it to Me" (Matt. 25:40). Jesus is in the giving and also in the receiving; we have disappeared. It's only Jesus. This is how it should be.

"You have not lived today until you have done something for someone who can never repay you." — John Bunyan

Select – *Write out the verse (or part of a verse) you selected.*

_____
_____
_____

Investigate – *What do you find in this verse?*

_____
_____
_____

Meditate – *What image comes to mind from the passage?*

Phrase – *What is the main theme or statement?*

_____
_____

List – *Actions you can take because of what you read*

_____
_____

Express – *Write out your prayer to God.*

_____
_____
_____

Glory & Grace

____/____/____ **Saturday**

Read Philippians 4
Read Focal Passage: Philippians 4:20-23
Memorize 4:6 and 4:13

Write out both Philippians 4:6 and 4:13 from memory.

_____
_____
_____
_____
_____
_____
_____
_____

Ever use a magnifying glass? It's wondrous to look at anything in such great detail. You can see things you normally would have missed without the magnification process.

"To glorify" (v. 20) is synonymous with "to magnify." When we magnify something, we make it appear bigger and clearer. We don't change the thing magnified, but we allow it to be seen for what it is.

Our lives are to glorify God—to magnify Him. As friends, family, and coworkers look at my life, they are actually looking through me to see what Jesus is like. The magnifying glass of my life must be kept clean, not for my own glory, but for the glory of my God. I don't want any smudges to distort the image others have of Jesus.

Paul wants this "unsmudged life" not only for himself, but also for the Philippians. That's why he extends grace to them (v.23). They must have the grace of God to be able to give glory to God.

Grace is but glory begun, and glory is but grace perfected.
— Jonathan Edwards

Select – *Write out the verse (or part of a verse) you selected.*

_____
_____
_____

Investigate – *What do you find in this verse?*

_____
_____
_____

Meditate – *What image comes to mind from the passage?*

Phrase – *What is the main theme or statement?*

_____
_____

List – *Actions you can take because of what you read*

_____
_____

Express – *Write out your prayer to God.*

_____
_____
_____

Group Study Guide

SIMPLE Peace may be used as a guide for a small group. Here is a suggested outline for the group sessions.

WEEK ONE: Preparation & Anticipation

Opening Questions: *The title of our study is* SIMPLE Peace. *Describe the most peaceful scene you can imagine. Is this a place you've been before or somewhere you'd like to go one day?*

Preparation

(See that each participant has his own book and Bible to use.)

Explain the process of the study to the group by reading aloud the *Why Study Philippians* section on page 5. You may have several participants read around the circle. Afterward, ask if there are any questions.

Say: *Each participant is expected to participate in at least the reading portion of the study. Some may choose to include the writing portion by answering the SIMPLE journaling questions each day. I encourage you to memorize the suggested verses as well. The more interaction you have with the text, the more life change will occur.* You are the judge of what you're ready to do; we want this group to be an encouragement for you to reach your personal goal for the study.

Ask: *Which one of the three levels of intensity do you feel you will choose, and why? Regular, Crispy, or Extra-Crispy?*

Explain the suggestions for the group by reading aloud the *Instructions for Your Experience* section on page 6. You may have several read around the circle. Afterward, ask if there are any questions.

Explain the SIMPLE journaling method for the group by reading aloud the *How to Use the SIMPLE Journal* section on page 7. You may have several read around the circle. Afterward, ask if there are any questions.

Anticipation

Ask: *Why did you want to participate in a study like this? What is your **motivation**?*

Ask: *What **changes** would you like to see in your life as a result of completing this study?*

Ask: *Explore the **possible barriers** by describing the one thing that may derail you from completing this study. Are you open to some suggestions from others in the group to help you overcome that barrier?*

***See you next week! We'll talk about what you've learned from* Philippians 1: The Stress of Life.**

WEEK TWO: The Stress of Life (Philippians 1)

Opening Questions: *Describe a time when you had overlapping commitments—when you had to be two places at one time. How was the situation resolved? How did you feel before it was resolved? ...after it was resolved?*

Ask the following questions allowing time for discussion. If the group is larger than 6-8, you may divide into smaller groups for these questions.

1. *How many were able to **read** 7 of the 7 days? Wonderful! What was the greatest difficulty for your consistency, and how did you overcome it?*

2. *How many chose to **journal** each day? Would one of you feel comfortable sharing something you wrote? Would another person care to share?*

3. How many were able to **memorize** the two verses? Would one of you feel comfortable quoting your verses out loud? Another person?

4. What was your **main takeaway** from this week's study? What did you learn about **God** or **yourself**?

See you next week! We'll talk about what you've learned from Philippians 2: The Example to Follow.

WEEK THREE: The Example to Follow (Philippians 2)

Opening Questions: *Describe a time when you got lost. It may be a funny story, or a scary story. How did you finally find your way, or did someone find you and lead you to safety?*

Ask the following questions allowing time for discussion. If the group is larger than 6-8, you may divide into smaller groups for these questions.

1. How many were able to **read** 7 of the 7 days? Wonderful! What was the greatest difficulty for your consistency, and how did you overcome it?

2. How many chose to **journal** each day? Would one of you feel comfortable sharing something you wrote? Would another person care to share?

3. How many were able to **memorize** the two verses? Would one of you feel comfortable quoting your verses out loud? Another person?

4. What was your **main takeaway** from this week's study? What did you learn about **God**, or about **yourself**?

See you next week! We'll talk about what you've learned from Philippians 3: The Motive to Continue.

WEEK FOUR: The Motive to Continue (Philippians 3)

Opening Questions: *Describe a time when you were frustrated and wanted to quit. What factors came into the decision to quit or continue on? What would you do differently today (if anything)?*

Ask the following questions allowing time for discussion. If the group is larger than 6-8, you may divide into smaller groups for these questions.

1. *How many were able to **read** 7 of the 7 days? Wonderful! What was the greatest difficulty for your consistency, and how did you overcome it?*

2. *How many chose to **journal** each day? Would one of you feel comfortable sharing something you wrote? Would another person care to share?*

3. *How many were able to **memorize** the two verses? Would one of you feel comfortable quoting your verses out loud? Another person?*

4. *What was your **main takeaway** from this week's study? What did you learn about **God**, or about **yourself**?*

***See you next week! We'll talk about what you've learned from* Philippians 4: The Peace of God.**

WEEK FIVE: The Peace of God (Philippians 4)

Opening Questions: *Describe a time when you felt alone. What did you do? What were the final results of this feeling?*

Ask the following questions allowing time for discussion. If the group is larger than 6-8, you may divide into smaller groups for these questions.

1. *How many were able to **read** 7 of the 7 days? Wonderful! What was the greatest difficulty for your consistency, and how did you overcome it?*

2. *How many chose to **journal** each day? Would one of you feel comfortable sharing something you wrote? Would another person care to share?*

3. *How many were able to **memorize** the two verses? Would one of you feel comfortable quoting your verses out loud? Another person?*

4. *What was your main takeaway from this week's study? What did you learn about **God**, or about **yourself**?*

End of Study Questions:

5. *What was your **main takeaway** from the entire four-week study? What did you learn about **God**? What did you learn about **yourself**?*

6. *You may choose to continue studying another book of the Bible using this format. **What will you do next?***

What? Memorize Scripture?

Alright, we've all heard the excuse before (as a matter of fact, we've all given this excuse), "I just can't memorize scripture!" You're in luck; I have the answer for that line: Phooey! Poppycock! No way, Jose!

We memorize things all the time. We can't fill up our minds like we fill up a pitcher of water. Our minds expand like a balloon the more we use them. The real problem is…we're just too lazy. Our minds are mush. They're not used to working hard for something.

Memorizing scripture is a spiritual and mental discipline. It's a lot like physical discipline. The more you train your body, the more strong and agile it becomes. In the same way, the more you train your mind, the more alert and responsive it becomes.

Also, as with training your body, better results come from a clear plan. I can help you with that too.

So, put some effort into it. Be purposeful in your spiritual discipline at least as much as you are in your other disciplined activities. Let's give it a try—whadayasay?

Here's a technique I've used for years to learn verses. It takes a little bit of effort in the beginning, but pays huge dividends in the end.

1. Go to the store and buy some lined 3x5 cards (like you have in that recipe box in the kitchen), a metal ring (the kind you can open and close to add more cards), and a hole puncher.
2. Get 3 or 4 cards together, punch a hole through them all in the top left-hand corner, and put the ring through the hole to connect them all into one packet.
3. Write the verse you're memorizing on the first card in this format: reference/verse/reference. It's important to write slowly and neatly (printing is my preference), concentrating on each word as you write it. This is the beginning of the memorization process.

> ○
> Ephesians 2:8-9
> > For by grace you have been saved through faith; and that not of yourselves, it is the gift of God; not as a result of works, that no one should boast.
> > Ephesians 2:8-9

4. On the back of the card, write only the reference. Then, once you memorize the verse, you can review by looking only at the reference side. This helps with "cheating." It may seem counter-intuitive but write the reference upside-down on the back. This will allow you to flip the card on the horizontal axis as you review it.

> Ephesians 2:8-9
>
> ○

5. Once you have the verse written, begin memorizing the verse from the end to the beginning; one word at a time. "The end to the beginning," you say? Most of us start at the beginning, repeating and memorizing each word in turn, causing us to say the beginning of the verse several times more than the end. So, as we proceed with repeating the memorized verse, it only gets harder as we proceed. If we memorize from the end to the beginning, the reverse is true: as we go from word to word quoting the verse, we proceed from the less repeated words to the more repeated words; thus making it easier as we go along.

6. As you memorize each word, picture that word in your mind before you go to the next one. I like to visualize each word in the same script that my elementary teachers used to write new words on the chalkboard; clear, clean white letters on a dark background. Maybe your favorite script is the Sesame Street block letters. Whatever works for you is fine, but visualize each and every word.
7. Memorize the verse word perfect; that's right, every "a," "of," and "the" in its place. This discipline will allow you to stay more focused and clear about the verse. If we memorize it generally, we'll only have a general recollection of the verse, so let's have word perfect memorization as the goal!
8. Carry this card pack with you wherever you go. I review verses while standing in line at the bank. If you put five minutes per day into this activity, plus add a few minutes of "wasted time" that we all have, it will change your life. Guaranteed!

In Conclusion

When I was in my twenties, I spent considerable time crafting my personal mission statement. It has served as the basis for all my decisions since that time. I've only altered it once in the 20+ years since.

My mission is to cause individuals to grow in their relationship with God through my active encouragement and by modeling a godly lifestyle [since 1993],
...and to influence others indirectly for Christ through something I've developed or someone I've influenced directly [added in 2007].

This book is my attempt to aid others no matter where they happen to be on their spiritual journey to take a few more steps toward Truth. I know I've had many people who have contributed to my own steps along the path; I hope to do the same for my readers.

I thank God He's put loving supporters into my life for this project. Thanks to friends Neal Korfhage and Betsy Yarborough, and to my daughter Mary Kathryn for reading for content and typos. Thanks to my son Mark for his many graphic and aesthetic contributions.

Thanks to my wife for life for reading and re-reading the manuscript. Her continual, unswerving support drove me to complete this project. I love her dearly.

Blessings to you all,

Steve Young
October 2014

Made in the USA
San Bernardino, CA
18 November 2014